a little like love

a little like love

payton olivia w

i started writing
for all of my lost love
and within that heartbreak
it was love
that i found

- payton olivia w

to my mum and my sister,
you have taught me all that there is to know about love

CONTENTS

lost

stay
stay
stay
my heart pounds with each breath
but the spaces in between
mumble that the leaving
is all i've ever known

in my dream you told me
i bought a house far away and made a home
but the truth is
nowhere felt as much of a home
as you did

there were times when my ache
was so loud
that i was scared to fall asleep
as that was the place
you and i would meet
so instead
i would lay my head down at the bottom of my bed
rest my feet on the pillow
pull my dog towards me
to feel some warmth
(maybe just to remind me unconditional love does
exist)
and with heartbroken tears
filling my eyes
i would trick myself into thinking
you can't fall asleep the wrong way around
of course he will come back
and once again
i fell asleep a fool

boys like you
are a dream
an everlasting adventure
of passion
danger and bliss
cigarette smoke
and french kisses
moonlight loving
naked bodies
and free souls
in the wild
of playful laughs
led by whiskey
and the burning stars
intertwining our humans as one
but the thing about dreams
is you eventually
have to wake up

you're the heartbreak i'm going to tell my kids

- when they don't know if they can pick
up their broken heart from the floor i'll say,
but your mumma did, so you can too
and this is when i'll tell them about you

witnessing the sunset tonight
reminded me of all your beauty
and in its darkness
i shed a tear

you used to ask me
*do you think that no matter where time takes us or
universes travelled, when we meet again will we always
have this spark?*

of course i replied, *a spark like ours doesn't just fade*

but as time tells
we can sometimes be wrong
you took our flame and ignited it with someone else

i still notice myself flinch whenever i hear the word love
because that word is now a synonym for gone

those nights you can't get comfortable
or fall asleep
that is what it was like in our love
i felt some sort of home
yet never quite belonged

he loves me he loves me not
he loves me he loves me not
he loves me
just not enough

i watched the sunrise this morning
and no matter where i went afterwards
i could still see those little orange dots
hazy but bright
and that is what it was like getting over you
i couldn't see you
but you were still always there

oh how i wish
for a time machine

to skip back to the moments
butterflies
awakened your stomach
at the sight of me

where the sheer thought
of my lips
brushing against yours
provoked the dance
of love and lust

to once more
recognise the knowing look
that promised
a richly magnificent life
of friendship on fire

your eyes telling me
to simply
fall
for your heart is already
halfway devoted to mine

could you fly back now, darling?
this time
i am ready to join you
for our butterflies to rest together

last night i dreamt of you.

we saw each other again but you were with someone else. you were happy and i asked if you were in love. before i could finish you replied with a smile, *without a doubt.* in the silence that followed you turned to me and asked if i could ever love you again. but this isn't what this is about. we were young. you were reckless and the stars don't write themselves. so i told you to go home to her. tell her you love her more than anyone else you've ever been with, this time, write your own god damn destiny. take it from a girl who has been there, if she loves you like she says she does, go hold her and don't risk letting her go.

when i woke up, silent tears filled my eyes so i shed a happy one for you.

it was my birthday and you sent me a text
you didn't say much but it was the first time i had heard
from you in months
my heart dropped when i realised
no one ends their text with
all the best
if they plan on picking it back up

and most of the time i feel like crying
but i have already cried enough
to fill the ocean
so
silently
i let the thoughts of you drown me instead

so darling don't wait up all night for them
because when you want them to chase you
they never do

they never do

i give up
if love wants to find me
it knows where i am

i cried myself to sleep for months
months on end of the feeling that my soul was being
ripped out and my eyes that could only half open from
all the tears

every night

so don't you dare try tell me that you were never good
enough for me
you were all i ever saw

if these walls could talk

they would be etched with your name
cobwebbed corners of our secrets
my hands pretending to be yours
and a splitting headache of all the dreams you have
disturbed

they would recite every poetry book
on my bedside table
stringing together the words of missing you
i scream into my pillow

if these walls could talk
they would crumble into ruins
with me gasping for air
buried at the bottom

i still think about you
i still see you when i look up to the night sky and
remember the love letter you wrote me telling me you
love me as much as you love the stars

but all they are, are balls of fire
billions of years old
which is maybe really a beautiful metaphor for our love
intense
magical and pure
we just witnessed it at the wrong time

so babe if you're reading this
i'll meet you again
in our other life
and this time we will burn brightly together

forever

every day
every day i dream of us together

and how grand of an adventure it could have been

maybe when you grow up we will meet again and you
will make me smile a little too big and laugh a little too
much
like you used to

- extract of a letter i will never send

can i tell you a secret?

i was really starting to fall for you

you were an echo in the distance
yet somehow
you got to me
bellowing through me
sweeping through my veins
but an echo is all you will ever be
a close parallel to my heart

i feel the seasons rush through me
and this sun has started to burn
even though i saw the cold coming
i didn't realise how warming
he had been

- the man who was the sun

i want to tell you that i miss you
but i don't need to say
that my heart aches for you
our souls used to dance together
so no matter if i tell you or not
i can still feel you occasionally swaying to our beat

you know i used to call it your side of the bed
but now it's just the other side
and it's lonely for you

so even though you can make me laugh like no other
and your eyes are a jungle i could get lost in
when i close mine i remember the last time i saw you
i see the back of you
and you see, my love
that breaks my heart a little more each time

our love was a calm storm
so when i look at the ocean
i think of us
and dream of our beauty
as if it never left

you told me you would keep me safe
away from the dragons
catch me when i fall
your big secure hands
always right there
warding away the dark nights and red apples
but the only thing i need saving from now
is the memory of you

i think as humans we love to complicate things
i go over and over our time together
i question everything
but i know you loved me
truly
and now
you don't
and it's really just as simple as that

they ask me about our love
so i tell them to think about the most beautiful sunset
they have seen
how you are stuck in a moment of time

as its bright yellow
changes so fast to a burning orange
the delicacy of the pink surprises you

in that exact moment you may believe in magic

but before you know it
the darkness arrives
and all these phases quickly end
so then they understand what it was like
to love
and be loved
by you

our love was like the ocean
vast
never-ending
intense

when we loved, we really loved
powerful
beautiful
magical
but when we argued, we really argued
raging and stormy

and unfortunately
no one can withstand
such deep waters

and that was just it
it was too hard
we loved
we loved
we loved so much

but love isn't meant to be that hard

the rise and fall
between the tide and rocks
the sun
the moon
dance of blue skies and rain
of my bruised heart
between

you

and

i

from my driveway in new zealand
i look up to the stars
and i pick out orions belt
i still see it
years later out of my window in the south of france
except it is upside down
this reminds me of you
of how i still see you
yet the image is somehow slightly different now too
so for one more night i fall into our lost love once again

and i think if someone asked me what i missed the most
i would say your laugh

it was slightly too loud
deep, a little awkward
but somehow slightly perfect

a little like love

remember that time we bought a scratchie and we won
$3
so like excitable children we bought another one only
for that to happen 3 more times
it felt like our luck was never going to run out

it's been a year now
and i'm sitting here by myself not feeling so lucky
anymore

and when our lips finally touched
everything felt like it fell into place
i didn't realise
for you
it tasted like a mistake

he will come

and spark something within you that you thought had
long been put out
you two will count the stars and thank the lucky ones
for each other
you will find what has been hidden deep within the
both of you
that together
creates something beautiful

then he will go

shooting stars
11:11
birthday wishes
and night-time prayers
are not meant to be used
on longing that he has changed
for if this is your wish
believe me when i say
forever is the only time you will wait

it was our third date
we were sitting outside by a park
and you were subconsciously playing with a stick
when you looked up at me
you asked if i wanted it
sure i said giggling
secretly putting it in my pocket when you looked away
i kept it in my car
thinking that months from now
when you buy me my first gift
i could say that it wasn't
that the stick was the first thing i ever kept from you
because on that third date
i knew you were someone special
but turns out you left
like the rest of them
and now i am left here
with a stupid stick
you won't even remember giving to me

i would do anything to be enough for you

some nights
my chest feels heavier
and to help me sleep
i trick myself into thinking
it is because
your heart is calling out to mine
both pulling towards each other
to the bottom of the sea
where all the best love stories lie

i was afraid of breaking your heart. when in reality all
these years later, whenever i see you, i break my own

- extract of a letter i will never send

it doesn't matter if you were here
nor there
you are always lost thoughts
swimming through my veins

you are all over me at the moment
but it's not the searing pain it used to be
i don't fall to my knees
nor does my stomach feel as though it's splitting in two
it's more of a dull ache
those moments i look up to the sun
content and warm
but still slightly empty without you

i write in pencil
and maybe this is because
i have never been used to things that stay

and i know it shouldn't break my heart
because you have already done that
but standing there
looking into those beautiful brown eyes
watching tears fall down your face
i realised that
maybe
my heart will always be
fractured for you

we are all just ants
scrambling around in our own busy little frantic lives
we forget how magical this real world is

i dream of a world
where we don't look in a mirror
and wish for something different
i dream of a world
with no *good lighting* and *choreographed selfies* of your
abs, jaw bones and plumped lips
i dream of a world
where *send nudes* is foreign
when unattainable is not the look we are all scrambling
to find, in too many self-destructible ways
where you don't get lost in a *swipe*
because everyone is too afraid
careless
to put in the effort required for the one thing we are
searching for
human connection
i dream of a world
we once had
but so effortlessly destroyed

we fell apart
and it broke my heart

our love story hasn't even started
but i already write the narrative
with heartbreak at the end of it all

- bad habits i am trying to break

being with you was like staring directly into the sun
an overwhelming sense of warmth
but the longer i looked
the blinder i became

you were a roller coaster ride. halfway through i would be screaming to get off but you were the adrenaline i kept chasing. no matter how many bruises my heart took. it came back. every time i would look into your beautiful brown eyes i knew i was doomed. for it was your magic power and your curse, the way you enchanted me. maybe it was written in the stars from the beginning for us to fail. but every shooting one we saw made us forget the rest.

- to the beautiful brown eyes

in this grand life we chose everything other than each other. i know it could have been the fairy-tale, somewhere deep in the forest, if we were brave enough to run wildly in. but the trail of all our wrong decisions ended as a smoking gun pointed at our hearts.

- to the friend

i was blind to every single person, other than you. you were my light and in the same instance the worst storm i have ever weathered. i would stitch up every open wound with love to show you just how beautiful you really are. your lips. your skin. your eyes. your smile. haunt me. as you are a ghost i would forever chase. a love too strong to break, but all too much. someone had to let go.

- to the sun

the little moments in life weren't so little with you. singing to the radio in the car. an ice-cream sundae at midnight. your laugh. your laugh was a sound i could listen to for the rest of my life. a sound that if anyone asked, i would tell them i'm a dancer and you, the music. a connection we didn't ask for but in all the wonderful ways the world answered for us. it was a dream of something greater. something we had both been waiting to come. a dream we both ended up having to wake up from.

- to the one with the laugh

as i re-read the love letters
you once sent to me
i break open
knowing the hurt will welcome itself
and settle beneath my rib cage
but maybe seeing these words
helps me heal
in a twisted way
a small reminder
our love was real

on and on
thoughts of you haunt me
but i am a new home now
and i will not welcome your ghosts

i look back
and i wonder how i ever saw so much love
when now i recognise
that i cried more than i ever had
the year i called you mine

and all of a sudden you are back
in the corners of my mind
hello my old friend
i would say it's a pleasure
but we all know you are the only one that ever found
lying easy
you try to smile at me
to make me feel something again
and i almost do
i almost fall back down the rabbit hole
aiming straight for your arms
i almost touch those perfect lips of yours
but my beating heart reminds me that i am worthy
of a love that will give me so much more
than yours ever could

out on the ocean
i look upon the land
and its vast magnetism
calling me home
but i have to close my eyes
because in that moment
i imagine i am floating back to you
and the pain washes over my body
until my exhale tells me
you have always belonged to the water, my ocean child
you deserve a love as deep as mine

i used to curse the night sky
for us not being together
now when i look at the stars
i thank them
upon the time of my life you were a part of

as the waves come and go
i thank my heart
for the time it loved you

and the time it let you go

looking out to the mountains
i see us
standing upon them together
and even though i don't know
where life has taken you over the years
i know in one of our lifetimes
those mountains
were conquered by our love

found

i am ready to love again
but they say the problem isn't whether or not you are ready to
love
it is if you are ready to be loved
if you see yourself as someone who is worthy of receiving love
i think this will always be a place where i get stuck
but i am ready to try
and isn't that enough?

i know you are tired
of letting people in
to your sacred
ground
your heart cannot seem to take a break
from all the visitors
who are gone by next week's morning
you are a home
and although
they can't quite see that yet
someone will come along soon
turn the lights on
make a tea
tuck themselves in beside you
and wonder why on earth
it took them this long
to find the place
they want to stay

i promised you the world
once we grew up
you discovered
i had only ever painted
the constellations
around you

- *love letter to myself*

i am starting to realise
it is ok
to give myself permission
to still miss you in those quiet moments
but to feel joy again
i am allowed to hold a space of grief for you
but this will never
never
hold me back from all the happiness
that is present
and still coming my way

one day you will be 16 and a boy with beautiful brown eyes will buy you a valentines rose. you will wonder if it's love, knowing it must be something, if every time you are near this one person, fireworks go off

one day you will be 18 and his beautiful brown eyes will look straight at you when he tells you he loves you. but later that night you will go home alone and cry in the shower knowing that if he truly meant it, you wouldn't feel this way

one day you will be 21 and you will fall in love with another beautiful brown eyed boy. this time you will know it is love but eventually he will break your heart too

one day you will be 23 and you will bump into the first brown eyed boy you fell for. you will daydream of how he could have changed in these past 7 years. but again, all that is left is sweet nothings and broken promises

today you will look in the mirror and see your ocean eyes looking back. knowing no matter how many beautiful brown eyes you fall in love with. you are here. still standing, promising the best is yet to come

in the midst of it all
the love for yourself
shall remain clear

a letter to myself

i forgive you for still being sad over him
i forgive you for letting yourself go every once and a while at
the surrender of him
for i trust your progress is a process that is ever changing
towards the light

years later i find myself
cuddled up on the couch
looking at my new lover
and it confuses me how many months
i spent trying to get over you

i used to trick myself into thinking
i would hear from you again
your voice playing like the devil's interval
through my nights
when i know now
it wasn't so much hearing your voice i missed
i just didn't know how to let it go

so i wallowed in my despair
with moments of light
that too easily scared me back towards the tunnel
you made me feel as though i was hard to love
that the next person would also lie so comfortably to my face
then silently mock me for believing them

but as these months turned into years
i sat on the thought
what if i was enough
what if the way i loved everyone else was the way i was meant
to be loved too

and as i let the ashes of your heartbreak scatter into the wind

i thank you for leaving
for leading me to myself
fully loved
fully accepted
and happier than i've ever been

maybe all we need is some good music, good company, and bad dancing to remind us of what it is to be alive

some friendships are simply sunshine
warm, comforting, beautiful
and after every night
it never makes you wonder
as you know when you wake up
their rays will be waiting to burn
brightly with you

you're my sunflower girl
side by side
we will bloom
with no fear
of ever being alone

you're my sunflower girl
for when i cannot find the sun
i turn to face you
and grow just as strong

you're my sunflower girl
teaching me
that magic is found
in the wild
that we are

you're my sunflower girl
with every petal
i can hear your whispers
of how bright life is
for we have grown together
and that is nothing short of a miracle

and it's true when they tell you
it's those who can still make you laugh

through it all

that make life worthwhile

no matter what stars we are under
or seas we have crossed
our souls dance together
certain that
friendships like ours
are destined to last

even when the sun goes down
and the rivers run dry
i will love you
my beating heart
will be right beside yours
until the seasons
decide to bloom again

they say paris is the city of love
but when i am there
i daydream about daisies
and coffee-stained mugs
graffiti love
stolen kisses
and fresh bedsheets

i imagine two lost lovers
brushing past each other on the metro
unaware
life's miracle just passed them by
i see a poet
followed by the poem
a thousand brushstrokes
and a million muses

as i sit
letting the wind ferociously blow my hair
into intertwined thoughts
of all these small moments
i skip by
hoping one day to return to

and you
you never came to mind

paris- the art of letting go

i want a lover like the ocean
his waves subtly reminding me
i am here
no matter where i drift
i will always be here

with you
it would be easy
a familiar star
strong heart
gentle eyes
i could see us years from now
cuddled on the couch
laughing at why we didn't collide sooner

collision course: you

goosebumps

when i look at you
with that smile
tempting me
telling me
come closer, i know you want to

the ocean is powerful
it moves you
yet makes you feel so serene in this moment
it crashes and rises and heaves and flows
yet never wavers
it shows us how to be resiliently strong
all the while having a force so soft it melts through you
it sparkles in the light, little diamonds whispering of its beauty
it shows off in the storms
raging in its magnitude that you can't tear your eyes off

the ocean is beautiful
and a little like you

find a partner that sees your light
a partner who is not intimidated by this brightness
someone that instead of backing away from the flames
sits right next to you
and softly whispers
burn baby, i am right here, witnessing you set this world alight

i make a wish on shooting stars
meditate in the forest and let the ocean cover me in calmness
i feel energies from crystals and howl to the moon
i let the sun soak up my anxieties and bathe in its beauty
and when he looks at me strangely i ask
how do you not believe in it?
you believe in us
and after all
we are all just made of the same thing

someone will come into your life
and they will see your kindness as a strength
match your love
and before you can
they will say

i've been looking for you
a home my heart can finally rest

i now get why they call it a soft spot for someone
my heart has no edges
and my mind
flows through every nerve of my body
every time
your eyes lock with mine

he had one of those laughs that made everything else
disappear

i want more nights of you singing in the shower
i want more nights being tangled up in bed like a pretzel
i want more nights full of cuddles and laughs
i want more nights and i want them
with you

you asked me what i was thinking
back then i was too scared to tell you

if you asked me now i would have said
i was thinking about how safe i feel with you
with your arms around me
i would have said out of the thousand stars we were looking at
i wished upon all of them, for you
i would have said if time could stop, i wanted it to stop right
then
i was thinking of all the possibilities that this vast universe has
to offer us
how we could star gaze together every night
and how i would feel safe for the rest of my life being in your
arms

- the night we stargazed up north

you were different
a dangerous smile
and kind heart
i was enchanted
from the first moment i met you
i knew something had happened
that i would follow you
through every forest
even carrying the fear
of getting lost

as you take my hand
and pull me away
running into the deep of the night
i find the brightest star
and softly confess
i bet you
right in this moment
my desires are burning brighter than yours ever have

the place of the world's edge
where the blues fade as one
where the infinite lies
and beginnings never end
this is where i will wait for you

every bone in my body
is telling me
it's safe
a gentle earth-shattering revelation
that i no longer need to prepare for the worst
for his love
is a safe place for me to land

i want to write about all of the lightness i feel when i think of
you
that when you're in my mind love is a word that comes first
but i don't quite know how

heartbreak
now that comes easy

and i realise how transformative that is
that you are changing the way i identify with love
and i can't think of anything more grand than that

they ask me to think about two things i couldn't live without
i think of how the mountains teach me strength and the
oceans show me freedom
that the stars will always lighten the darkness
the feeling of belonging as i return to my motherland
knowing my growth has been sown through all the countries
travelled
but then i laugh to myself
as if i even have a choice
because those two things
have chosen me
love
+ you

it's strange to think of all the different little moments that paved their way for us to find each other. that now there is a place in my heart that will always be yours. a place filled with laughter and kindness. of music and dancing. a feeling that everything will be ok in this world. a sense of warmth. a calmness that having fun is the most important thing of all. i will count my lucky stars they led me to you. thank you for trusting me, believing in me and loving me.

they used to tell me that home wasn't a place but a person
and it wasn't until i had nowhere to go
but the arms of those i loved
i fully understood
it didn't matter if the world was crumbling to pieces
if i was with these people
i was home

and my worries all of a sudden
seemed to float above me
a gentle
yet certain release
that i am someone
who is easy to love

he blurs my thoughts with a cloudless sky of my favourite
colour blue

which is to say
he doesn't really fog my mind at all
with him
all i see is the sun

and i can't quite believe
when i look up at you
that you are mine

and i can't quite understand
that the love i have always been searching for
has found a little corner in my heart
that belongs to you

i am starting to realise
that i will have your arms to come home to
for the rest of my nights

and i don't quite know what to do with that
except allow your tenderness to sit
within the depths of my bones
to let it kiss away my scars
and flow through my veins
until all i will ever bleed
is my love for you

as i stare into his eyes
he smirks and says
you're looking at me like you're in love or something
and my heart didn't know
whether to burst outside of its chest
or quietly sigh a breath of thank you
to every little path i have ever taken
that has led me here
so instead it did both
knowing it will be safe here
within his heart of a home

what a different yet calming thought
that for the rest of all the cold nights
and rising suns
i will be held by you

through all the storms
the moon winked to the ocean
relishing in the fact
that this time
they got it right

they would ask me where my favourite place is
expecting me to say a country or city
my traveller's heart has fallen in love with
but my mind would only circle back
to being in your arms
and how that's the only place i ever want to be

there is something so gentle
so comforting
in knowing this world conspired
for us to live in the same lifetime

if i could
i would scale
every rockface
to show you
that being in love
and being brave
are one and the same
and i'm willing to be
both with you

you had said there was always something about me. between us. at the beginning i didn't believe you. but as the years went by, the moon could no longer hold our secrets and sent a star to collide before us. that first kiss, we both know it shouldn't have happened like that and maybe we jinxed ourselves to be doomed from the start. there was a golden thread holding us together, that had been slowly pulling us closer, our gravities had no choice but to become one. we became a whirlwind of passion, curiosity, and love. and suddenly it made sense. our souls had already danced together, our bodies had just finally caught up.

- to the dancer

i hope you know
that there is not a single star in the night sky
who hasn't heard about the immense love
i hold for you

if the earth crumbled to a million pieces tomorrow, would you know that you have the same effect on me? that the simple touch of your fingers tracing down my spine sends a ripple of shivers through my bones and the way your arms hold me, i could collapse into a world that fits just the two of us. that when your hand encompasses the side of my face, i imagine my jawline as the ocean and your thumb as the shore that never leaves. would you know that i have always felt a calling to the sea and looking into your eyes i finally understand why. that i see art within you, which is to say a life with you is one we are all searching for. of mystery, understanding and desire. would you know, that now whenever i try to write about love, you are all that i can see.

i would sit in the palm of your hand
and see the world at your fingertips
following your lead through this mess
convincing myself we know the direction
when the truth is we could run wild
and it wouldn't matter
as long as we were together

i hope you know
that i would go through
every heartache
tribulation
and hurt
my soul had to go through
all over again
if it meant finding you

golden hour

a souvenir
of your beauty

golden hour

and as maui did
i would use everything in my power
to slow down the sun
if it meant longer days
to love you

a kiss is just a kiss

unless it's under a thousand stars

and with you

a kiss is just a kiss

i see sunshine within him and it only makes me want to run into his love even more

right from the start
you never made me question where i stood
thank you
thank you for bravely
yet so effortlessly
never making me doubt our love

he is worth all the stars
in the night sky
and i will thank them
for leading me straight into the gentlest
yet strongest arms
i've been carried by

and what a rare and magical thing
it is to feel as though your heart
has finally found a soft place to land

the way he says my name makes me believe that every star
has conspired for us to love
that they shine down undoubtedly letting us know that
loving each other is the easiest decision
we have ever had to make as we roam this earth

hemmingway once said
all you have to do is write one true sentence
write the truest sentence that you know
and all i can think about
is how much i love you

and in the chaos of life
there is you

i look at you in awe
in everything you embody
you are the sculpture
the painting
the poem and dance
i see art within you and i love how that makes me see the world

you are my saviour
and i don't just mean you protect me
i mean when my whole world
comes shattering down
you are there

you are always right there
loving my pieces
back together

they say when you know you know
and i have spent my whole life questioning
until the day
that i met you

my protector, i promise to thank the stars every night for you
you are all i have ever been searching for
an electric soul and gentle heart
my biggest adventure and home all in one

- to the one who changed it all

ACKNOWLEDGEMENTS

to my sister for always encouraging me, inspiring me and paving the way for me to follow in my twenty-six years. as well as being my editor. to my mum, you are it. you are love. thank you for holding me through every single one of my heartbroken nights. to b, for changing the way i see romantic love. to my family and friends, you know who you are, thank you for filling my life with so much joy. my life is so full because of you all. to my grandma, as the tui sips on your honey-made water we will hear her song and think of you. to the instagram writing community, for your endless support and kindness. and lastly, to all of you. my readers. thank you from the depth of my heart for sharing this love.

payton lives bravely from her heart. art has always led the way, and as she grows and navigates each new chapter in life, she discovers new art forms that best allow her to live her truth. while poetry has now taken centre stage, dance was her very first love.

she finds freedom in expressing passionate depths through the written word. writing is her safe space, where she can heal, make sense of inner and outer worlds and find threads of love woven through all that she experiences.

payton is most at home by the ocean and surrounded by family and friends. give her art, the sun, the beach, furry four-legged friends and a circle of those closest and dearest, and her heart will be forever full.

a little like love is her first poetry book. you can find her on instagram: @p.o.wpoetry and at her etsy store: powpoetryandprose